LESSONS FROM THE WRITING WILDERNESS

How I answered, prepared for, and survived the journey to become a Christian author—and how you can too!

A 21-day devotional & study guide

Jeaninne Stokes

Contents

INTRODUCTION

Are you being called to the ministry of writing?

Then get ready to begin a journey to prepare yourself for the ministry that awaits you. History is replete with examples that show when God called people to do great things for Him, they first spent time in the wilderness preparing for their respective callings. For example, Moses spent time in the wilderness to get ready to lead the Israelites out of Egypt. Joseph spent time in the wilderness to get ready to become second in command in Egypt. Jesus even spent time in the wilderness before He was ready to begin his ministry to die for the sins of the world.

In twenty-one bite-sized lessons, this book chronicles my journey to live out my call of writing and to become a Christian author – beginning with the day I heard and answered the call to pursue a ministry in writing and left my "Egypt" to prepare, the lessons I learned as I spent time in my "wilderness" preparing for my writing ministry and the challenges I had to overcome while there, and the moment I finally reached my promised land and became a Christian author.

Why did I write this book? Because maybe God is also calling you to the ministry of writing and you'd like help for how to begin your new journey. If this describes you, it is my hope my story will provide you the inspiration and information needed to help you prepare for the work of writing God is giving you to do.

How can you benefit from this book? By answering the study questions at the end of every lesson. Questions for individual reflection or group discussion are included to encourage you to dig deeper as you begin your journey of writing to become a Christian author.

Ready to begin? Then join me as I share these twenty-one lessons from the writing wilderness to help you answer, prepare for, and survive your journey to write for the kingdom!

Section I

ANSWERING THE CALL TO WRITE FOR THE KINGDOM

LESSON 1

LISTEN TO THE STIRRINGS WITHIN

It was by faith that Moses, when he grew up, refused to be treated as the son of Pharaoh's daughter. — Hebrews 11:25

How is life changing for you today as a Christian writer? Are you finding that which you once found pleasure in waning and your desire to write more growing? Does this desire to write seem to envelope your heart, mind, and soul more and more than ever before?

Moses, the great leader of the Israelites, was born an Israelite but grew up as an Egyptian. As a young child, he enjoyed the luxuries that came with living his life in Egypt, but as he matured into a young man and saw the burden of slavery on his people, the Israelites, his desire for what he once enjoyed in Egypt began to wane.

Life began to also change for me as a Christian writer while living in my Egypt. Like the influential leader Moses, I enjoyed the luxuries that came with living my life. I was married to a wonderful man, had two beautiful children, and enjoyed a budding career. I loved the rhythm of getting up every morning to begin a good day's work, dressing for success, kissing my husband goodbye, and making the journey to work.

But as the years rolled by, a change began to occur within me as writing began to consume my thoughts. I arrived for a day's work but sometimes spent my mornings writing rather than preparing for my workday. I began exploring ways to get the poetry I had written as a hobby for years published. And one night, while praying, I heard the Lord whisper, "Jeaninne, you will publish a book when you are forty." I was thirty-nine.

Yet, since I still had a job to do, I dismissed the stirrings within to write more as just a passing thought or phase. Until the day I was offered a promotion on my job that I had been waiting to receive and found myself saying: "No, thank you" because the passion to pursue my existing career that once burned brightly in my life was slowly dimming.

Dear writer, if life as you know it has been changing and a greater desire to write more is stirring within, be careful not to dismiss what is happening to you as a passing thought or phase. For it may be the work of the Holy Spirit stirring up a desire within you to use your writing gifts and talents in a greater way – a greater way to impact the world.

Are you paying attention to the stirrings happening within?

Study questions for personal or group discussion

1. How is life changing for you as a Christian writer while living in your Egypt? Are there any new passions stirring with you to do more as a Christian writer that were not there before?

2. Are you noticing any signs while living in your Egypt that indicate God may want you to use you in a greater way as a Christian writer? What are they?

3. What do you see as the greatest challenge while living in your Egypt that would keep you from stirring up the new passion within you to write more for the kingdom?

LESSON 2

ANSWER THE BURNING BUSH

When the Lord saw he had gone over to look, God called to him from within the bush, "Moses! Moses!" Exodus 3:4.

In what way is God calling you to write for the kingdom? Has he told you directly through a voice from the sky? Or through a sermon that seemed like it was written just for you? Or through a friend who told you how much your writings minister to him or her?

I remember the day I heard the call. The voice was so crisp and clear in the morning air that I turned in my parking lot at work to see who was there. I saw no one, yet clearly I knew I had heard someone say, "Jeaninne, it's time to go."

Yet knowing how much I needed my job, I kept working and wrote when time allowed.

A year passed and I convinced myself the voice I had heard that day in the parking lot was just a figment of my imagination, until one day, a colleague stopped by my office and shared the following words:

"Jeaninne, I stopped by to say goodbye. My husband has given me the opportunity to stay home to raise our children, and I wanted to stop by to say goodbye before I left." After bidding her farewell, I closed my door and wept, envying her for taking a step I wanted to take, but did not yet know how to do.

As I wept, I heard the voice of the Lord speak again. "Will you trust Me? Will you give up your career and trust me to meet your needs?"

My decision rested on that one question. Would I trust God? We could not afford to live on my husband's salary alone, and I provided health insurance for my children and myself. Would God really take care of my family if I quit?

I thought about Abraham. God told him to leave everything–his home, family, and friends–and travel to an unknown land, and He promised He would bless Abraham and make him the father many nations. Without question, Abraham walked away from the secure life he loved and knew because he believed God's promise of a greater blessing. How I wanted an unquestionable faith like Abraham exhibited—a faith willing to leave my job because God had told me to do so, even when I wasn't sure all of the reasons yet for why He was asking me to go.

Dear writer, if you believe God is calling you to the ministry of writing, has the time come for you to heed the call and step out to do more with your gifts as a Christian writer? Then I encourage you to take a step of faith, if necessary, to begin your writing journey. Faith that says: "I am willing to answer the call, Lord. Use me. Use me to write for your kingdom."

Study questions for personal or group discussion

1. Do you believe God is calling you to a ministry of writing? Why or why not?

2. Answering the call to write for ministry may require you to step out of the comfort zone of your life in some way. Is there a step of faith God is wanting you to take today to answer the call to write for ministry? What is it and how will Abraham's step of faith help you to take yours?

3. Read Isaiah 6:1-8, How does Isaiah's call and response to the Lord help you answer your call to write for ministry?

LESSON 3

GO GET YOUR BLESSING

"With your permission, Moses said, I would like to go back to Egypt to visit my family." "Go with my blessing, Jethro replied."
— Exodus 4:18

Before you answer the call of writing for ministry, whose blessing do you need to receive?

With the major life change I was being asked to make to leave my career, it was important I received my husband's blessings. So, one night during dinner, I broached the topic in conversation with Him.

"Honey, I have something to share with you. I keep hearing God telling me to quit my job. I can't explain all the details yet, but I've received several signs showing he wants me to resign."

"But why? Why would God tell you to quit when he knows we need your job to sustain our lifestyle? We cannot afford to live on my salary alone."

"I don't know, and I admit it makes little sense to me either, but I can't erase the fact that I keep hearing God telling me it's time to go."

"Well, if God told you to go, who am I to stand in the way?"

In a devotion from the book, *Great Days with the Great lives,* best-selling author Charles Swindoll writes, "When God is nudging you in a new direction, it is important to be sensitive about how you communicate that call to others. Do not assume they know all you know about the process. Do not expect them to greet the idea with immediate acceptance and open arms. Communicate your thoughts with tenderness, care and understanding and give them the courtesy of time to think things through."

Dear writer, if you have answered the call of writing for ministry, when you are ready to share your new calling with those you desire to receive a blessing from, remember to heed the advice shared by Dr. Swindoll in communicating your new calling to others. For it will take a village to help you live your calling as a Christian writer - a village that starts with the blessings of those nearest and dearest to you.

Study questions for personal or group discussion

1. Whose blessing is it important for you to receive before you answer your call to write for the kingdom? Why?

2. Write a plan for how you will ask for the blessing of the person named above with tenderness, love, and care. Include the date, time, and place of when you will carry out this task.

3. What will you do if you do not receive the blessing of someone especially important to you? Will you still proceed?

LESSON 4

IT'S OKAY

But Moses protested again. "What if they won't believe me or listen to me? What if they say, 'The Lord never appeared to you'?"
— Exodus 4:1

What do you do when you tell others about the new direction God is leading you as a Christian writer, but their reaction is not quite the way you would like it to be?

I encountered this issue regarding my call to write for ministry the day I told some of my colleagues I was quitting my job. Here were some of their comments:

"Are you sure?"

"Is this what you and your husband agreed to when you got married?"

"Aren't you aware how hard it is to get the kind of job you have?"

"Nobody makes a living as a writer. Are you sure you can?"

God told Moses to lead the Israelites out of Egypt. But Moses did not think the Israelites would believe what God had told him to do. He doubted they would believe God had called him—a former Egyptian—to deliver them from the Egyptians. He wondered whether they would believe God would ask him—a man who stumbled over his words—to speak before a great Pharaoh on their behalf.

Christian author Micah Maddox said it best in her article: *When you question your calling*. "People won't always agree. They will not always cheer you and they might even let you know how much they do not approve; but they are not the one calling you. When in doubt, do not worry. Trust the one who called you."

Dear writer, whether your call to write for ministry is a call to step away from a promising career or to clear your calendar so you can devote more time to writing, will you also trust the one who is calling, even when others may not yet believe?

Study questions for personal or group discussion

1. Despite what anyone else believes, write down how you know for sure God is calling you to a ministry of writing?

2. Read Acts 2:29. Explain what it means to you as to why others may not understand or support your reasons for taking a step of faith to answer your call to write for ministry?

3. Jesus proceeded with his calling to save the world from sin, despite others' unbelief in what God had told him to do. What does he teach you about answering your call to write for ministry even when others may question what God has told you to do?

LESSON 5

HE IS WITH YOU

So Moses took his wife and sons, put them on a donkey, and headed back to the land of Egypt. In his hand he carried the staff of God. — Exodus 4:20

Are you being asked to leave some of the comforts of your Egypt to answer your call to write for ministry, but you are feeling a little shaky because you do not have much to stand on except a belief that God has told you to go?

I can relate.

After resigning from my job, my colleagues threw me a lovely good by party. But after the hugs and tearful goodbyes were shared and the boxes had all been packed, all that remained on my office walls were a few nails and the outlines of plaques, degrees, and other certificates once displayed to remind me of the hard work I had invested in my career. As I prepared to leave my office for the very last time, everything was tightly packed except one item. My doubts. They still swirled around in my mind like a whirling tornado:

Did I make the right decision? Were some of my colleagues right when they said I was making a mistake in giving up my career? Should I have switched to another type of full-time job that still offered me medical benefits, rather than giving up my career altogether?

Beautiful memories also rushed to mind as I sat reflecting on my working years. I recalled the day I drove by my office building and knew it was the very place I wanted to begin my career after I completed graduate school. I remembered the friendly faces that welcomed me when I entered the building for the first time. I thought of the friendships I had established and the joy of working alongside people who wanted, like me, to make a difference in the lives of students.

I also remembered the bad times. The daily stress that came with managing an office with limited money and staff; students who didn't always appreciate the advice given to help them succeed; bosses who sometimes wanted more than I could give; and the emotional stress I experienced when my department downsized and I almost lost my job.

What was the common item I carried through the good and bad times of my career? My staff. The staff in the form of my old office Bible. When I needed strength, I leaned upon the Word; when I needed guidance, I leaned upon the Word; when I needed comfort, I leaned upon the Word.

Dear writer, if you believe God is also calling you to say goodbye to some of the comforts of your "Egypt" to answer the call to write for ministry, do not be afraid of what lies ahead. For as long as you have an assurance of your calling and the staff of His Holy Word, you can begin your new journey knowing He is with you every step of the way.

Study questions for personal or group discussion

1. Sometimes God requires us to leave our comfort zones and take a step of faith to begin preparing for our writing ministries. Is there anything God is asking you to leave behind today to begin preparing for yours?

2. If you are being called to leave something behind in your life to begin preparing for your writing ministry, how will you lean on the Holy Word for support, guidance, and strength to carry it out?

3. What assurance does Psalms 119:105 offer you as you launch out to begin preparing for your writing ministry?

Section II

PREPARING TO WRITE FOR THE KINGDOM

LESSON 6

EXPECT TO WANDER

They said to Moses, "Why did you bring us out here to die in the wilderness? Weren't there enough graves for us in Egypt? What have you done to us? Why did you make us leave Egypt?" — Exodus 14: 11.

What do you do if you give up some of the comforts of your life in your Egypt to prepare for your writing ministry and life is not going as expected? Do you keep trusting in God's new plans for your life as a Christian writer, or do you return to the comforts you had in your Egypt?

These were questions that arose after I quit my job and life was not going as expected at home. Instead of taking a morning stroll with my preschooler as I had planned, I drove her to daycare. Instead of volunteering at my son's school, I parked my car in the garage, so no one knew I was home. After spending my first weeks home in a whirlwind of cleaning, I longed for the intellectual stimulation of work and the office conversations of my colleagues.

As the days slowly turned, life went from bad to worse. I struggled to pay our bills and began depleting our savings account to fill in the gaps. After zeroing out our savings, I moved to using our credit cards to pay bills. Our debt soared.

Desperate for answers, I prayed, "Why, God?" Why did you tell me to quit my job and then allow so much havoc to occur in my life after I obeyed? Did I not hear you correctly? Did I make a mistake?"

I sounded just like the Israelites after their miraculous deliverance from Egyptian bondage. After 400 years of slavery, God heard their cry and sent Moses to deliver them. And when Pharaoh made one last attempt to bring them back and they were trapped between the Red Sea and hundreds of Egyptian soldiers, they told Moses they would rather have stayed in Egypt than die in the wilderness.

Dear writer, if you have left some of the comforts of your life in your Egypt to prepare to write for ministry and life is not going as expected, there will be days when you will long to return to what was. But don't, because God still has great plans for you. Just like He opened up a path of deliverance for the Israelites, He can open up a path of deliverance for any problem you encounter. So keep trusting in His new purpose for your life as a Christian writer, even when it will feel at times like you are wandering in the wilderness.

Study questions for personal or group discussion

1. In what ways do you feel like you have been sent into the wilderness since launching out to prepare for your writing ministry?

2. What do you believe the lessons are God wants you to learn as a Christian writer while you are in the wilderness preparing for your writing ministry?

3. Read Jeremiah 29:11. How will this verse help you to keep trusting God's promises for your life as a Christian writer when life is not going as expected?

LESSON 7

BELIEVE IN YOURSELF

Now go, for I am sending you to Pharaoh. You must lead my people Israel out of Egypt. — Exodus 3:10

As you prepare for your call to write for ministry, have you found yourself questioning whether you have the qualifications needed to fulfill the call God has given you, even to the point of telling God he has chosen the wrong person? The wrong writer?

You would not be the first writer to do so.

I have always been an early riser, but one morning something woke me earlier than usual, but I dismissed the disturbance and went back to sleep. The next morning, I was awakened early again. This time I heard an audible voice–one I am certain was from the Lord– sharing these words, "get up and go into your office."

With only a small lamp shining through the early morning darkness, I obeyed. After reaching my home office, the voice spoke again. "Open your Bible. Read the story of Moses and his call to deliver the Israelites from Egyptian bondage. Write in your journal everything you are learning about his journey.

As I read about Moses' journey, the Lord kept speaking. "I asked you to read about Moses' journey because you are about to embark on a similar one. I am calling you to the ministry of Christian writing and you will be home for a season to prepare for it. During your season of preparation, you will question your ability to live out your calling because of the challenges you will experience along the way. These challenges will tempt you to turn back to your former career. But just like I took care of Moses and the Israelites and helped them reach their Promised Land, I will also take care of you and help you become the Christian author I am calling you to be. All I ask is that you trust me along the way."

"But me, Lord? Are you sure I am the one you are calling to write for ministry? Writing for me has always been a hobby I pursued while chasing after my career. How can I write for publication when I have no formal training in writing? Are you *sure* you've chosen the right person?"

"Yes, I have chosen the right person, my child. And because I am calling you, I will equip you for the task of writing I have called you to do."

Dear writer, just like God promised he would equip me for the call of writing for ministry, He will equip you too. So when you question your qualifications, remember that you are the one. You are the one he wants to use to write for the kingdom!

Study questions for personal or group discussion

1. In what ways are you protesting your call to write for ministry?

2. Read the following Bible stories of the following people called by God to do special tasks for Him. What can you learn from the lives of these men and women regarding how God will equip you for your call of writing for ministry, especially if you do not feel qualified to do it?

   > Noah
   >
   > Moses
   >
   > Joshua
   >
   > Esther

3. According to Ephesians 3:20, in what ways does the Holy Spirit qualify you to write for the kingdom?

LESSON 8

WAIT FOR YOUR INSTRUCTIONS

You must build this Tabernacle and its furnishings exactly according to the pattern I will show you. — Exodus 25:9

What instructions has God already given you for your writing ministry? Is he calling you to write devotions? Teaching articles? Short stories? Christian fiction? Who does he want you to reach with your writing ministry?

These were the questions that swirled in my mind once it became evident God had called me to write for ministry. Since I was not sure how to proceed with the preparation process for my new calling, one night I prayed, "Father, since you have called me into the ministry of writing, show me how. How do you want me to carry out this call of writing you have given me to do?

Like the putting together of a beautiful piece of tapestry, God answered my prayer. First, he gave me the name for my writing ministry. Next, He explained the format he wanted me to use, the different components he wanted me to offer, and the platform he wanted me to use for my writing ministry. Last, he capped off His instructions by giving me two scriptures—Jeremiah 29:11 to remind me of his plans for my writing ministry, and Habakkuk 2:3-4 to remind me not to expect my ministry to bloom overnight, but it would grow in a slow and steady manner as I completed the work of preparation he gave me to do.

Dear writer, if you need to know how God wants you to flesh out your writing ministry, do not be afraid to ask and then wait for Him to make clear what the instructions are he wants you to follow. Is he calling you to write devotions to teach God's Word in a short and captivating way? He will make His instructions clear. Is he calling you to write short stories that convey a message of inspiration and hope? He will make His instructions clear. Is he calling you to write romance novels that show others how to honor Him in their dating and marital relationships? He will make His instructions clear. Each person's call as a Christian writer is specific to the instructions God gives them. So go ahead and ask God what his instructions are for your writing ministry. Then get ready to build your ministry according to his plans for you.

Study questions for personal or group discussion

1. What is the vision God has given you for your writing ministry? What instructions has he already given you to carry out the vision? Write them both here.

2. Purchase a large poster board and create a collage of the vision God is giving you for your writing ministry. Then place it in a conspicuous place to remind you of God's purposes for you as a Christian writer.

3. Explain how Proverbs 29:18 will help you stay motivated and focused on the vision God has given you to do as you prepare for your writing ministry?

LESSON 9

STOP PRAYING - GET MOVING!

Then the Lord said to Moses, "Why are you crying out to me? Tell the people to get moving! Pick up your staff and raise your hand over the sea. Divide the water so the Israelites can walk through the middle of the sea on dry ground." — Exodus 14:15

An unknown philosopher once said, "Sometimes we know what to do, but we pray for more guidance as an excuse to postpone doing it." Does that describe you? Are you still praying for more guidance for how God wants you to prepare for your writing ministry when He has already given you His instructions on what he wants you to do?

I found myself doing just that one day. Six months after quitting my full-time job, I was scheduled to return to work as a part-time employee, but after I understood my purpose for why I was home, I did not want to return. One day I laid prostrate on my kitchen floor, praying for God to offer a way for me to stay home instead. But no matter how earnestly I prayed, all I heard were the following words: "Get up and return to work."

The story is told of a deeply religious man on top of his roof because of rising floodwaters. A man came by in a helicopter to rescue him, but he told the man in the chopper he was waiting on God to rescue him. The next person came by in a rowboat, but the man said, "No thanks, I'm waiting on God to rescue me." A third person came by in a canoe and he told that person the same thing, "No thanks. I'm waiting on God to rescue me." The man drowned. When he stood before God, he asked, "Why didn't You save me when I prayed?" God responded, "I sent a helicopter, a rowboat, and a canoe. Why didn't you use them?"

Dear writer, like the man on the roof, be open to how God wants to deliver you from any problems you encounter as you prepare for your writing ministry. Even when His deliverance is not packaged in the manner you would like, that package may be the very thing you will need to prepare for the work of writing God has called you to do.

Is it time for you to stop praying and get moving?

Study questions for personal or group discussion

1. What has God already told you to do to prepare for your writing ministry that you are not doing? How will you activate your faith and move forward in doing what God has already told you to do?

2. Brainstorm a list of resources you already have that you can use to resolve any problems, financial or otherwise that may arise as you prepare for your writing ministry.

3. What does the story of Rahab found in Joshua, Chapter 2 teach you about using your resources to resolve any problems that may occur in your life as you prepare for your writing ministry?

LESSON 10

LET GO OF YOUR RIGHTS

It was there at Marah that the Lord set before them the following decree as a standard to test their faithfulness to him. — Exodus 15:25b

It's true. You have the right to live your life the way you want to live it. But what if God asks you to relinquish some of your rights to prepare for your writing ministry?

This was a choice I was faced to make one day as I prepared for my writing ministry. Before quitting my full-time job, my boss and I had agreed I would get paid a salary commensurate with my experience and qualifications when I returned to work part-time. But the day I contacted her to let her know I was ready to return to work, she shared the following words:

"Unfortunately, I can't pay you the same salary you had before you resigned since you are returning to a different job. Are you still interested in the position?"

I immediately thought about Paul. When God called Paul to preach the gospel, he gave up some of his rights to live out his ministry. Paul sacrificed his right to live comfortably, the right to marry, and the right to get paid for his labor. Paul could have kept the rights he deserved; yet he laid them down so he could live out the ministry God had called him to do.

Dear writer, the call to write for ministry may require you to lay down some of your rights too. On one hand, God could ask you to give up a promising career to prepare for your writing ministry, or something as simple as relinquishing the right to sleep late on Saturday. Whatever the right God asks you to relinquish, may you, like the apostle Paul, consider it rubbish in comparison as you prepare for the new work of writing God has for you to do.

Study questions for personal or group discussion

1. Name at least one rights you believe God wants you to give up to help you prepare for your writing ministry? What do you believe he wants you to relinquish this right? two.

2. Read I Corinthians 9. Make a list of the rights the apostle Paul gave up so he could be free to preach the gospel to the Gentiles. Compare Paul's list to your list in question one. What did you learn?

3. Read Philippians 2:5-8. How does Jesus' example of relinquishing his rights encourage you to relinquish any rights you may need to give up so you can prepare for your writing ministry?

LESSON 11

LOOK FOR THE MANNA

Then the Lord said to Moses, "Look, I'm going to rain down food from heaven for you. Each day the people can go out and pick up as much food as they need for that day. I will test them in this to see whether they will follow my instructions." — Exodus 16:4

How can you prepare to write for ministry if you cannot afford to purchase the resources you need? That's a question I asked myself after quitting my job because I knew I had very little discretionary income to buy the resources needed to learn my craft, sign up for writing classes, or attend writing conferences.

Yet, like the faithful God he was to the Israelites in providing Manna as they trekked across the wilderness on the way to their Promised Land, each time I awoke to begin the work of preparation for my writing ministry, there it was: His "manna." For example, one morning while searching the Internet, I found a support group for Christian writers located only a few blocks from my home. Another day I visited a discount bookstore in my neighborhood and purchased several affordable books on the craft of writing. When I needed a computer for my home office, my husband brought one home from work he no longer needed. When I wanted to attend my first writer's conference, the coordinator of the conference—who also was the director of my critique group—allowed me to attend at a discounted rate.

Philippians 4:19 states, "And this same God who takes care of me will supply all your needs from His glorious riches, which have been given to us in Christ Jesus." (NLT)

Dear writer, I can testify that the promise of Philippians 4:19 rang true in my life as I prepared to write for ministry. And just as God provided his manna for me, he will provide it for you too. All you have to do is trust him to meet your daily needs and you will find it there every morning - His manna to help you prepare for your writing ministry.

Study questions for personal or group discussion

1. Make a list of the things you believe you will need to prepare for your writing ministry. For example, books to study the craft, computer equipment, money for writing conferences, etc.

2. Name some ways you have already seen God provide for your needs as a Christian writer?

3. How will you stand on the promise found in Matthew 6:33 that he will continue to provide for all of your needs as you prepare for your writing ministry?

LESSON 12

HE WILL USE IT ALL

Then Moses told the people of Israel, "The Lord has specifically chosen Bezalel son of Uri, grandson of Hur, of the tribe of Judah. The Lord has filled Bezalel with the Spirit of God, giving him great wisdom, ability, and expertise in all kinds of crafts. — Exodus 35:30-31

Have you ever wondered what would happen to your previous skills and qualifications in your old career if God is calling you to prepare for a new career as a Christian writer? Will they still be used? Or discarded?

I wondered if my former skills and qualifications would be discarded as I prepared for my writing ministry until I took a closer look at the apostle Paul's calling. Paul's background included being trained as a Pharisee. He had such a strong zeal for his Jewish beliefs that he hunted, persecuted, and killed Christians. Yet, when God called Paul to become a missionary to the Gentiles, God did not discard any of Paul's former qualifications; instead, he used every single one.

There was no reason to believe God would do any less with the skills and experiences I had gained while working in my former career. In fact, I realized my array of skills and qualifications may have been the very reason he chose me. For God saw someone who already had a love for learning and who would use those same qualities to learn how to write. He saw someone who enjoyed inspiring and teaching students, and he knew I would use those same skills to inspire and teach people through the medium of writing.

An unknown philosopher once said, "God does not waste our time nor our skills; instead, He will use our past and present so we may serve Him with our future."

Dear writer, whatever skills and qualifications you already offer as you prepare to write for ministry, bring them all to the table of preparation, confident in knowing that God will not waste any qualifications you have acquired, but will use them all for His kingdom use.

Study questions for personal or group discussion

1. In what ways has your background already prepared you for your writing ministry?

2. How did Moses and Paul's background prepare them for their respective ministries? What does this say to you about how God will use your background of experiences to prepare you for your writing ministry?

3. Make a list of the skills, experiences, and other credentials you have acquired. How do you see God re-channeling your existing skills and experience into your new ministry as a Christian writer?

LESSON 13

FIND YOUR ARMOR BEARER

"I can't carry all these people by myself! The load is far too heavy!" "I will come down and talk to you there, I will take some of the Spirit that is upon you, and I will put the Spirit upon them as well. They will bear the burden of the people along with you, so you will not have to carry it alone." — Numbers 11:14, 17

As you prepare for your writing ministry, who is the person you would like to have as your armor bearer—that person to lean on when the weight of your calling at times gets too heavy to bear? That person who will pray for you and hold you accountable to achieve your writing goals?

I found my armor bearer one day in an unlikely place.

While eating a snack during a workshop break during a writing conference, I noticed a young woman decked out in a lovely white pantsuit. She was casually reading the conference brochure. After a moment's hesitation, I walked over to meet her.

"Hello, my name is Jeaninne. What's yours?"

"Cynthia. Nice to meet you."

"You, too. Is this your first time attending the conference?"

"Yes, what about you?"

"No, it's my second."

"What made you come back?"

"I returned because each time I come, I gain something beneficial to help me become a better writer. What about you? Why are you here?"

"I'm here because I want to write a Christian book and a friend recommended that I attend this conference to learn how."

"Since we have similar goals, why don't we commit to holding each other accountable to ensure we achieve them?"

"I'd love to!"

Dear writer, just like I found my armor bearer that appointed day at my conference, you'll need an armor bearer to hold you up as you prepare for your writing ministry. It will need to be someone who prays and intercedes on your behalf regarding your writing needs and concerns, someone who encourages you not to give up on your writing calling when the journey gets hard, and someone who holds you accountable to reach your writing goals.

So be open to the promptings of the Holy Spirit when he encourages you to call that distant friend, or to say hello to a perfect stranger. For that person may be the very one God may use as your armor bearer.

Study questions for personal or group discussion

1. Why is it important for you to have an armor bearer as you prepare for your writing ministry? What does Jonathan's relationship with his armor bearer in I Samuel 14:6-13 teach you about the qualities you need to look for in an armor bearer?

2. Make a list of the qualities you would like to have in your armor bearer as you prepare to write for ministry.

3. Based on the qualities you listed in question number two, who are two people you would like to ask to serve as your armor bearer?

LESSON 14

KEEP A RECORD OF YOUR PROGRESS

At the Lord's direction, Moses kept a written record of their progress. — Numbers 33:2a

What if a major test or trial occurs in your life as you prepare to write for ministry? Would it stop you from preparing for the work of writing God is calling you to do, or would the difficulty propel you forward?

This was a question I had to resolve the day I received a distressing call. A call that came early one morning.

I had visited my doctor for my annual women's checkup, and he noticed some unusual calcifications from my last mammogram. After sending me through a battery of tests, I was told to expect a call in a week with the results. When the doctor called, I heard the startling news.

"Jeaninne, I'm sorry to inform you, but the results from your tests show you have breast cancer."

"Breast cancer?" "Are you sure?"

After sharing my fears about my diagnosis with a friend, she responded, "Did you ever think that you received this diagnosis, not as a death sentence, but to help you prepare for your writing ministry? Getting breast cancer could be God's way of helping you practice your craft as you begin your treatments and chronicle your new journey—a journey others may benefit from one day when they read your story."

What my friend shared made sense because that is exactly what God told Moses to do. Before he and the Israelites began their journey through the wilderness to get to their promised land, God reminded Moses to keep a written record of their progress along the way. And because he obeyed, millions of people benefit today from reading their story.

Dear writer, in his best-selling book, *The Purpose Driven Life,* author Rick Warren states that we have a storehouse of experiences in us that have been gained through every test and trial we have experienced, and God wants us to eventually share the lessons we have gained from those experiences. So take time to keep a record of the storehouse of lessons you are learning every day on your life journey, because someone is out there waiting to read your story.

Study questions for individual or group discussion

1. Based on James 1:3-4, how will the tests and trials you experience as you prepare for your writing ministry add depth to your writing?

2. How has journaling your personal struggles through the years helped you find solace and comfort? How will it help you find solace and comfort through any new trials you encounter as you prepare for your writing ministry?

3. Are you in the midst of a trial right now? How do you think God wants to use it to help prepare you for your writing ministry?

LESSON 15

YES, YOU'RE A MINISTER

Use this oil also to anoint Aaron and his sons, sanctifying them so they can minister before me as priests. — Exodus 30:30

Christian writer, did you know that you are called to be a minister of the gospel of Jesus Christ and writing is to be the pulpit you use to preach the gospel? It took me a while before I accepted that I was a minister until I read an excerpt from the following article by author Denise George: In the article, *"The Writing Minister: How to Expand your Ministry to the World,"* published in The Christian Index, July 2016, she writes:

As you already know, the world is a hurting place, and people need instruction, wisdom, encouragement, and hope. As a minister, you have the answers for the world's hurting and confused people. Not only can your book help a person now, but the written word has lasting power, leaving a legacy that will continue bearing rich fruit long after your time on earth has passed.

Since I still had my doubts, another helpful message arrived in my email box one day to help confirm my role as a minister:

"Jeaninne, thank you for your devotions. They are always so inspiring, and I appreciate how you know just what to say to meet my need for the day. I enjoy a nice cup of coffee and look forward to reading your devotions as part of my morning routine."

I had given my reader a word of encouragement and hope. The same words my pastor gave me every Sunday. I had no reason to doubt anymore if I was a minister for the article and email had made it clear: I was a minister and writing would be my pulpit, my special place to share God's answer for a lost and hurting world.

Dear writer, oftentimes a minister is defined as someone who stands in a pulpit on Sunday to preach God's Word. But as a Christian writer, never forgot that you are also a minister, called to "preach" and share God's answer for a hurting world from the pulpit of your pen and pad. Jesus has given you all the authority you need to write for the kingdom, so go, write, and make disciples for Him.

Questions for individual reflection or group discussion

1. How do you believe God wants to use your pulpit as a Christian writer to make a difference in the world?

2. How will you appropriate the commandment found in Matthew 18:18-20 to "go and make disciples" using your writing pulpit?

3. What is the issue that concerns you the most that you believe God wants you to write about on his behalf?

LESSON 16

IT TAKES TIME

When Pharaoh finally let the people go, God did not lead them along the main road that runs through Philistine territory, even though that was the shortest route to the Promised Land. — Exodus 13:17a

In what ways does God need to strengthen your faith, improve your writing skills, and build your character to get you ready to write for ministry? For me, the answer to those questions was, "A lot."

After I left my career to prepare for a career as a Christian writer, I expected to immediately publish a book, get listed on the New York Times bestsellers' list, and appear on *The Oprah Winfrey Show.*

But none of those things happened because it was not time. Before I could publish a book, I needed to improve my writing skills. I needed to take writing classes and attend writers' conferences. I needed to immerse myself in reading books on how to write and develop the discipline required to write professionally. I needed to learn how to receive constructive criticism to improve my writing. I needed to grow in my relationship with the Lord.

For these reasons, I spent several years in the quiet obscurity of my home with no one else applauding my efforts and worked hard to become the writer God called me to be.

In his book, Going Places with God: *A Devotional Journey Through the Lands of the Bible,* author Wayne Stiles states:

"The long way seems like the wrong way and, like the Hebrews, we become impatient because of the journey. Yet when we look back in hindsight, we come to appreciate how God used the journey - and all the victories and failures along the way – to prepare us for something we felt ready for much earlier."

Dear writer, it will take time to develop your craft as a writer, learn the writing industry, and develop your character as you seek to become the Christian writer God is calling you to be. So do not get discouraged with your preparation process when it seems like it is taking longer than expected, because the time God is investing in you is not just designed to get you ready; it is designed to get you *completely* ready for your writing ministry.

Study questions for personal or group discussion

1. In what ways do you need to prepare yourself for your writing ministry?

2. In what ways does God need to test your faith and refine your character so you can be ready for the ministry of writing he is preparing you to do?

3. Read Habakkuk 2:3. How will the words found in this scripture encourage you when it seems like it is taking a long time for you to prepare for your writing ministry?

Section III

ENTERING THE LAND OF WRITING FOR THE KINGDOM

LESSON 17

GET READY TO BREAK CAMP

*When we were at Mount Sinai, the Lord our God said to us,
"You have stayed at this mountain long enough. It is time to break
camp and move on."* — Deuteronomy 1:6-7a

What is the one thing that would stop you from submitting your writings for publication, even if you knew the time had come for you to do so? Fear? Self-doubt? Procrastination?

I received approval from an author friend to send a proposal to her publisher, but a week later my manuscript still sat in a file on my computer. Why? Because I was afraid to break camp. I had camped for so long in preparation mode to become a Christian author that I had gotten comfortable. I was comfortable writing with zero rejection. I also wasn't sure I wanted to surrender control of my manuscript to a traditional publisher who might change the contents into something I had not envisioned. In addition, I was not ready to hear the words, "Sorry, but we don't think your manuscript meets our needs for publication at this time."

Although the Israelites spent several years in the wilderness, they did not remain there forever. After the first generation died because of their unbelief and the second generation was old enough, the time came when they broke camp and entered their Promised Land.

Dear writer, there will come a time when you have learned everything you need to learn during your preparation process. You will have studied and practiced your craft and established a writing routine; you will have researched the markets; you will have grown in your knowledge of God's Word and in your relationship with Jesus Christ. So when the time comes when you have prepared long enough, don't be afraid to break camp and move on to the next leg of your writing journey.

Study questions for personal or group discussion

1. What are some of the warning signs that may occur in your life as a Christian writer that indicate it is time for you to "break camp?"

2. Make a list of the fears you need to overcome that may keep you from submitting your writings for publication when the times comes for you to do so?

3. Read Joshua 1:9 and I Timothy 1:7. How will these scripture verses help you overcome your fears listed above so you can move forward with submitting your writings for publication?

LESSON 18

IT'S OKAY TO EAT THE CORN

You must not muzzle an ox to keep it from eating as it treads out the grain. —Deuteronomy 25:4

For profit or for free? How do you plan as a Christian writer to offer the books you write and publish for your intended audience?

I faced this dilemma as I prepared to publish my first book. After sharing my concerns with a good friend, she replied, "There are many Christian authors who profit from their writing ministries. Take, for example, Pastor T. D. Jakes. Pastor Jakes draws income from his best-selling Christian books that inspire and encourage millions of readers. For these reasons I see nothing wrong with you profiting from your books, but the important thing is for you to decide if this is what you believe God wants you to do."

During biblical times, as the oxen worked, the Israelites wanted to muzzle their mouth to keep the oxen from eating the corn as they trampled the grain. But Moses reminded his people it was okay for the oxen to eat because they were the ones who labored to ensure the corn turned into grain.

Dear writer, like the oxen, when you have labored during your preparation process to ensure you provide quality writing for the audience God has called you to reach, and when the time comes for you to publish your books to share with your intended audience, proceed with confidence, knowing it is okay to eat the corn.

Study questions for personal or group discussion

1. Look up two Christian authors you admire and their annual book sales. How will their sales as Christian authors help you reconcile any concerns you have about profiting from the books you write and publish as a Christian author?

2. Read I Corinthians 9:11. Explain what this verse means as you plant spiritual seeds into others through the books you write and publish?

3. How does I Timothy 5:18 apply to you as a Christian author when it comes to profiting from the books you will write?

LESSON 19

TAKE IT – IT'S YOURS!

Caleb tried to quiet the people as they stood before Moses. "Let's go at once to take the land. We can certainly conquer it."— Numbers 13:30-31

What do you do when you finally overcome your fear of rejection and submit your manuscript to a publisher for review but your manuscript is not accepted for publication? Do you give up on your dream to become a Christian author or try again?

After practicing the craft of devotional writing for several years as I prepared for my writing ministry, I finally broke camp and submitted three devotions for publication to a devotional market, hoping one of them would get accepted. The email arrived, and to my chagrin, they had all been rejected.

Twelve spies were sent into the land of Canaan to explore it. Each saw the same magnificent land, but when they also saw the giants who inhabited the land, they did not believe they could conquer it. However, one of the spies, Caleb tried to encourage the people to take the land because he believed he could conquer it.

Because he believed, he eventually received his portion of the Promised Land.

Dear writer, experiencing rejection will be part of the journey of becoming a Christian author. And when rejection occurs, you will have to decide how you're going to view it. Will you view the land of publication as a land you can conquer by continuing to trust in the quality of your writings and submitting them again until your manuscript is accepted, or as a land you cannot conquer because you have allowed rejection to discourage you from trying again.

Like Caleb, the "giant" of rejection does not have to defeat you if you keep believing in the quality of your writing and that you have what it takes to become a Christian author.

Study questions for individual or group discussion

1. Experiencing rejection will be a part of becoming the Christian author God has called you to be. How does Jesus' response to rejection found in Matthew 13:54-58 help you deal with rejection when it happens to you?

2. Joshua and his army obeyed God's orders to walk around the city of Jericho seven times until the walls came tumbling down. No matter how many times your manuscript is rejected for publication, how will the strategy given to Joshua and his army encourage you not to give up?

3. Who are two successful Christian authors you know who experienced rejection? How did they overcome rejection? How will they help you overcome it?

LESSON 20

KEEP GOING!

And they said to Moses, "Why did you bring us out here to die in the wilderness? Weren't there enough graves for us in Egypt? What have you done to us? Why did you make us leave Egypt?
— Exodus 14:11

Now that you are day twenty of this book and have read about the lessons I learned while on my journey to become a Christian author, are you feeling tempted to continue writing as a hobby rather than professionally? Are you thinking that the journey to become a Christian author may be something too hard for you to accomplish?

I understand. Many times, I wanted to give up on my journey too, so much so that one day I began looking for a full-time job to return to my former career. But each time I applied; strange things occurred. Once, I was told the employer never received my application although I had an email from Human Resources saying otherwise. Another time I was told I did not meet their "special" qualifications, even though all of my qualifications matched the needs of the job description.

Frustrated, I prayed, "Father, I know I'm qualified and sometimes overqualified for every job I've applied for. Why do I keep getting turned down?"

"My child, could it be these doors of employment aren't opening because I'm closing them? Could it be I want you to keep moving forward on your journey to write for ministry full-time like I have called you to do?

After being delivered from Egyptian bondage, the Israelites began their journey through the wilderness towards the special land God had promised them; yet when they saw Pharaoh and his army in the distance marching toward them like a great army of ants, they told Moses it would have been better if they had never left Egypt. However, the Israelites did not really want to return to Egypt and the cruel bondage which they had just received deliverance from; they just did not want to die in the wilderness either.

Dear writer, during those moments of your journey when you are tempted to turn back to the comforts of writing as a hobby, remember the plans he has for you. Plans to use your writings to instruct, inspire, and encourage. Plans to use your writings to share his answer for a hurting world. So keep moving forward with the call of writing he has given you to do, until you reach your promised land!

Questions for individual reflection or group discussion

1. Make a list of the things that would tempt you to give up on your calling to become a Christian author? How will you work hard to overcome these temptations when they occur?

2. What doors are currently closing in your life to let you know God wants you to keep moving forward on your journey to become a Christian author?

3. Read Isaiah 40:29-31. When challenges arise and you are ready to turn back to writing as a hobby, how will this verse encourage you to keep going on your journey to become a Christian author?

LESSON 21

YOU WILL ENTER THE LAND

So the people crossed over opposite Jericho. —Joshua 3:16-17

Elation. Joy. Sheer bliss. Those were all the feelings that ran through my body the day I opened the package from Federal Express and saw my first book. I had labored for months and months to write this book and I was finally holding it in my hands.

And still, that first book almost didn't happen. As I have shared throughout this book, my journey to become a Christian author was riddled with many challenges along the way—challenges that included personal, financial, and health issues. At times, those challenges caused me to want to give up on the call of writing and to become a Christian author.

Despite the many times I wanted to quit, I kept hearing the sweet voice of the Lord whispering in my ear to keep writing. He encouraged me to keep writing during those days I didn't feel like writing; to keep writing when I doubted if my writing would ever be good enough for publication; to keep writing when I battled discouragement, doubt, and disappointment.

Because I kept writing, in 2008, I finally achieved my goal and became a Christian author. And my career as a writer did not stop there. After my first publication, I published four more books, and am currently working on my fifth.

A wise but anonymous philosopher has said, "The road to success is not straight. There is a curve called failure, a loop called confusion, speed bumps called friends, caution lights called family. You will have flats called jobs. But if you have a spare called determination, an engine called perseverance, and a driver named Jesus, you will make it to a place called success."

Dear writer, these are the lessons from my journey. As you begin your journey to become a Christian author, it is my hope that each lesson inspires you, no matter what the challenge, to never give up on the call of writing God has given you to do. For just like God began and completed his good work in me to become a Christian author, he will do the same with you. In fact, the Bible tells us that when God begins a good work in us, we can be confident He will bring it to completion (Philippians 1:6, paraphrased). So continue to remain faithful to the ministry of writing God has given you to do, until the day you enter your promised land!

Study questions for individual or group discussion

1. According to Romans 11:29, the gifts and calling of God are irrevocable. What does this verse mean to you as you seek to become a Christian author, despite the challenges you have encountered along the way?

2. Read Philippians 1:6. Do you believe if God has started a good work of writing in you, he can help you bring it to completion and become the Christian author he called you to be? Why or why not?

3. Read I Thessalonians 5:24. In what ways has God already been faithful to you on your journey as a Christian writer? How does his prior faithfulness grant you confidence that he will help you enter your promised land to become the Christian author he has called you to be?

APPENDIX 1

HELPFUL RESOURCES FOR CHRISTIAN WRITERS

Books about the craft:

A Christian Writer's Manual of Style. Updated and Expanded Edition by Robert Hudson. Zondervan, 2004.

Writing for the Soul, by Jerry B. Jenkins. Writer's Digest Books, 2006.

How to Write What You Love and Make a Living at It, by Dennis Hensley. Shaw Books 1st edition, 2000.

An Introduction to Christian Writing, second edition by Ethel Herr, Write Now Publications, 2000.

The Little Style Guide to Great Christian Writing and Publishing, by Leonard G. Goss and Carolyn Stanford Goss. Broadman & Holman Publishers, 2004.

Understanding the Christian Nonfiction Book: From Concept to Contract, by David Fessenden, Sonfire Media, 2011.

Write that Devotional book: From Dream to Reality, by Lee Warren. Midnight Latte Publishing, 2015.

How to Write for the Christian Marketplace, Kindle Edition, by Jo Huddleston and Vicki Phelps, 2012

The Art and Craft of Writing Christian Fiction, by Jeff Gerke.

The Complete Guide to Writing the Christian Novel, by Dr. Penelope Stokes.

On Writing, by Stephen King, Scribner; Anniversary edition, 2010.

On Writing Well, by William Zinsser. New York: Harper Perennial, Anniversary reprint edition, 2016.

Stein on Writing: A Master Editor Shares His Craft, Techniques, and Strategies, St. Martin's Griffin, 2000.

The Elements of Style, Fourth Edition, William Strunk, Jr., Longman Publishers, 2000.

Books for the writing life:

The Writing Life. Annie Dillard, Harper Collins Publishers, first edition, 1989.

Bird by Bird. Some instructions on writing and life. Anne Lamott. Anchor Books, 1995.

Write His Answer – A Bible study for Christian Writers. Marlene Bagnull. Write Now Publications, 1999.

The Successful Author Mindset. A handbook for surviving the writer's journey. Joanna Penn. Curl Up Press. 2016.

Books for locating or finding an agent, editor, or publisher:

The Christian Writer's Market Guide 2020: Your Comprehensive resource for getting published. Steve Laube, Christian Writers Institute, 2020.

TRAINING FOR CHRISTIAN WRITERS
Christian Writing Conferences
(https://writing.shawguides.com)
Roaring Writers (roaringlambs.org)
The Christian Communicator
(christiancommunicator.com)
The Christian Writers Institute (stevelaube.com)
The Jerry Jenkins Writers Guild (jerryjenkins.com)
Write His Answer (writehisanswer.com)

WRITING ORGANIZATIONS
American Christian Writer's Association
(regaforder.wordpress.com)
American Christian Fiction Writers (acfw.com)

WRITING CRITIQUE GROUPS

World-wide Christian writers critique groups
www.meetup.com/topics/christian-writers-critique-group
Faith Writers Online Critique Group
www.faithwriters.com/critique-circle.php

WRITING BOOK PROPOSALS
Jane Friedman (janefriedman.com)
Jerry Jenkins (jerryjenkins.com)
Michael Hyatt (michaelhyatt.com)
Terry Whalin (terrywhalin.com)

WRITING TOOLS
MasterWriter (masterwriter.com)
ProWritingAid (prowritingaid.com)
Scrivener.com (scrivener.com)

EDITING SERVICES
Affordable Christian Editing
(www.affordablechristianediting.com)
Michelle Chester, EBM Professional Services
(www.ebm-services.com)
Elaine Flowers (Beforeyoupublish.com)
Marilyn Bradford Editing (Bradfordm@icloud.com)
Scribendi Religious editing and proofreading services
(scribendi.com)
The Christian Pen (thechristianpen.com)

MANUSCRIPT SUBMISSION SERVICES
ChristianBookProposals.com
Writersedgeservice.com

TRADITIONAL CHRISTIAN PUBLISHERS
Baker Publishing Group (Bakerpublishinggroup.com)
Barbour Publishing (barbourbooks.com)
B&H Publishing (bhpublishinggroup.com)
Dove Christian Publishers
(dovechristianpublishers.com)
Faith Words (faithwords.com)
Harvest House (harvesthousepublishers.com)
Intervarsity Press (Intervarsity.org)

Moody Publishers (moodypublishers.com)
NavPress (navpress.com)
Thomas Nelson (thomasnelson.com)
Tyndale House (Tyndale.com)
Waterbrook Multnomah (WaterBrookMultnomah.com)
Zondervan (Zondervan.com)

CHRISTIAN SELF-PUBLISHERS

Book Baby (Bookbaby.com)
Christian faith Publishing
(Christianfaithpublishing.com)
Inspire Books (Inspire-books.com)
Lulu (Lulu.com)
WestBow Press (Westbowpress.com)
(Xlibris.com)
Xulon (XulonPress.com)

SELF-PUBLISHERS

Ingram Spark (Ingramspark.com)
Kindle Direct Publishing (Kdp.amazon.com)

APPENDIX 2

TEN COMMANDMENTS FOR CHRISTIAN WRITERS

I will acknowledge God as Lord of my life and the one who called me to write for ministry.

I will keep my relationship with God a priority in my life as a Christian writer.

I will not worship my writing ministry but keep it in its proper place in my life.

I will not use the Word of God in a negative or derogatory way as a Christian writer.

I will take time to worship and rest to re-energize myself, so I have the energy to write effectively as a Christian writer.

I will not allow my writing ministry to take priority over my family.

I will remain faithful to my calling and overcome any temptations or distractions that seek to keep me from doing the work of Christian writing.

I will not steal the ideas or writings of others and use them as my own as a Christian writer.

I will write to inspire, educate, equip, or inform and never to hurt or harm anyone as a Christian writer.

I will not envy the success of other Christian writers but focus on living out the race of writing God has given me to run.

APPENDIX 3

A WRITER'S STATEMENT OF FAITH

I have strength for all things in Christ Who empowers me—I am ready for anything and equal to anything through Him Who infuses inner strength in me, [that is, I am self-sufficient in Christ's sufficiency]. (See Philippians 4:13, AMP.)

I will write with all the strength and energy that God supplies, so that God will be glorified. (See 1 Peter 4:11, TLB.)

I will write not in my own strength, for it is God who is all the while effectively at work in me—energizing and creating in me the power and desire—both to will and to work for His good pleasure and satisfaction and delight. (See Philippians 2:13, AMP.)

My strength must come from the Lord's mighty power at work within me. (See Ephesians 6:10, TLB.)

In Him in every respect I am enriched, in full power and readiness of speech (to speak—and write—of my faith), and complete knowledge and illumination (to give me full insight into its meaning). (See 1 Corinthians 1:5, AMP.)

Now I have every grace and blessing; every spiritual gift and power for doing His will are mine during this time of waiting for the return of our Lord Jesus Christ. (See 1 Corinthians 1:7, TLB.)

I actually do have within me a portion of the very thoughts and mind of Christ. (See 1 Corinthians 2:16, TLB.)

I can be a mirror that brightly reflects the glory of the Lord. (See 2 Corinthians 3:18, TLB.)

I will commit everything I do to the Lord. I will trust Him to help me do it, and He will. (See Psalm 37:5, TLB.)

I will lean on, trust and be confident in the Lord with all my heart and mind and choose not to rely on my own insight or understanding. (See Proverbs 3:5, AMP.)

I will commit my work to the Lord, then it will succeed. (See Proverbs 16:3, TLB.)

Writing is my work, and I can do it only because Christ's mighty energy is at work within me. (See Colossians 1:29, TLB.)

I will be strong and courageous and get to work. I will not be frightened by the size of the task, for the Lord my God is with me; He will not forsake me. He will see to it that everything is finished correctly. (See 1 Chronicles 28:20, TLB.)

I need to keep on patiently doing God's will if I want Him to do for me all He promised. (See Hebrews 10:36, TLB.)

I am convinced and sure of this very thing, that He who began a good work in me will continue until the day of Jesus Christ—right up to the time of His return—developing [that good work] and perfecting and bringing it to full completion in me. (See Philippians 1:6, AMP.)

His mighty power at work within me is able to do far more than I would ever dare to ask or even dream of—infinitely beyond my highest prayers, desires, thoughts or hopes. (See Ephesians 3:20, TLB.)

Compiled and paraphrased by Marlene Bagnull. Reprinted with permission.

ABOUT THE AUTHOR

Jeaninne is a Christian author and Bible-teacher called to teach God's Word through the medium of writing. Along with writing and publishing her books on her own ministry platform, *Inspiration for Living Ministries,* she is the founder of *Writing for Him Ministries,* where she provides personal coaching, workshops and speaking engagements to help aspiring writers answer the call to write for ministry and Christian publication.

Besides this book, she is the author of *Living by Faith: A Collection of Inspirational Poetry; Baileyisms: Inspirational Quips and Quotes for Living the Christian Life;* and *Living by Faith: An Adult Coloring Book of Inspirational Poetry.* Jeaninne's writings have also been published in *Cross and Quill, The Christian Communicator,* and *Christian Woman Today* Online.

If you are an aspiring Christian author, subscribe to Jeaninne's email list to receive a weekly word of inspiration for your writing journey at: https://www.writingforhim.org/join-my-mailing-list.

You will also receive notifications about her newest books, workshops, and classes for Christian writers.

If you found this book helpful as you begin the journey of writing for ministry, please consider leaving a review on the site where you purchased your copy.

Follow Jeaninne on Facebook -
https://www.facebook.com/jeaninne.stokes/
and Twitter - https://twitter.com/Jeaninne_Stokes,
and visit Jeaninne via her website:
www.inspirationforliving.net